Naughty Nicky's book

CW01021515

Read about:

Linda   Linda's mummy   the baby

Robert   naughty Nicky   Uncle Dick

Loppy   Hammy   the firemen

1

One day Linda was going
to school by herself.

She met the postman
at the pillar box.
She met a big girl with a puppy.

She saw a bus with a **5** on it.
She saw men working on the street.

She went past some shops.
She went past the ice cream van.
She came to Hill Street.

She saw Tommy's mummy
at the bus stop.
She saw Karen's daddy in his car.
She saw the milkman on the street.

She had to cross the street
and she went to the lollipop lady.

The lollipop lady had a big lollipop.
It was red and yellow and black
and it had

STOP

CHILDREN   on it.

The lollipop lady went
on to the street with her lollipop.

A black car had to stop.
A red bus and a big lorry
had to stop too.

The drivers saw the writing
on the lollipop.

Linda crossed the street
and she went into school.

She told her teacher
she came to school by herself.
She told the teacher she saw
a big girl with a puppy
and a postman with letters.

She said some men were working
on the street.

Robert had a picture
of his uncle Dick.
Uncle Dick had a little monkey.

The children liked the picture
of the monkey.
Robert told them
the monkey's name was Nicky.

Linda made a shop in school.

The shop had

bread	potatoes	sausages
books	postcards	comics
milk and lollipops.		

The children all came
to look at Linda's shop.

8

milk

books

Ben came to the shop
and he got potatoes and
a comic from Linda.

Robert came and he got
sausages and bread.
The teacher got milk and a book.

They all liked Linda's shop.

The children had a rabbit in school.
His name was Loppy.

Loppy had a big box
with his name on it.
Robert put some food in the box
and Shaleen put some milk.

The children liked to play with Loppy.

Hammy

The children had a hamster in school.
Her name was Hammy
and she had a box
with her name on it.

Hammy liked to sleep in her box.
Linda and Ben came
with some food for her.

Hammy and Loppy were happy
in school.

Linda's mummy came to school.
She had the baby with her.

She saw Linda in school
and she met Linda's teacher.

She saw Linda's writing.
She said it was very good
and Linda was very happy.

She saw Linda's reading book.
The name of the story was:
  The Happy Bears.

She saw Linda's shop.

Linda let her mummy see Hammy.
They took Hammy out of her box,
but she was very sleepy.
So they put her back in her box
to sleep.

Uncle Dick came to school
with Nicky.
All the children stopped working
and they came to see
the little monkey.

Suddenly Nicky got away
from Uncle Dick.
He jumped on to Linda's shop.

He spilled the milk
on the comics.
Then he put the sausages
in the milk.
Next he put the postcards
in the milk too.

Uncle Dick shouted:
   "Stop, you naughty monkey,"
and he took Nicky away.

15

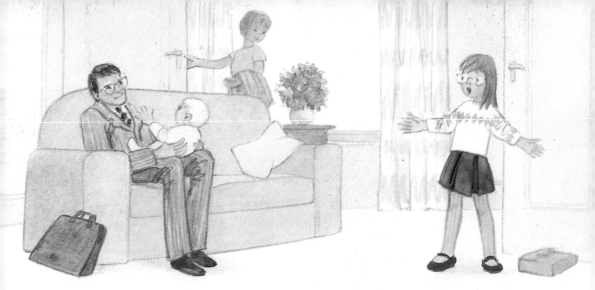

Linda went home with her mummy
and the baby.

Linda told her daddy
about naughty Nicky.
She said Robert's uncle came
to school with Nicky.
She said Nicky jumped on her shop
and he made a mess of it.

Her daddy said:
 "What a naughty monkey."

Robert was going home from school
with his mummy
and they saw a shop on fire.

They saw a red fire engine
going to the fire.
The fire engine had firemen in it
and it had a ladder.

It stopped at the fire
and the firemen got out.

The firemen put up the ladder.
One of them went up the ladder
with a hose.

Another fireman went
into the shop
with another hose.

They put lots of water on the fire
and the fire went out.

The firemen put the hose back
on the fire engine.

They took down the ladder
and they all went
into the fire engine.
Then the fire engine went away.

A police car came along the street
and a policeman got out.

The policeman said:
"Where is the fire?"

Robert's mummy said:
"The fire was in the shop
but the firemen put it out."

Robert said:
"The firemen came very fast.
They put lots of water on the fire
and it went out."

Robert saw some of the water
in the street.
He started to play in the water
and he fell.
He got very wet.

His mummy said:
    "Get up, you silly boy,"
and they went away home.

They met Robert's daddy
on the street.
He was coming home from work.

Robert told him about the fire
and the fire engine.
He told him he fell into the water.
Robert's daddy said:
  "Silly Robert,"
and they all went home for tea.

Robert had a big brother.
His big brother was working
away from home.

Robert was writing a letter to him.
He was writing the letter
on yellow paper.

He told his brother about
the fire and the fire engine.
He told him about the rabbit.

Then Robert went out with his mummy
to post the letter.

Robert's big brother got the letter
and he was very happy.
He said:
  "I must get a postcard
  for Robert."

He sent Robert a postcard
with a fire engine on it.

Uncle Dick made a cage
for Nicky.

He said:
  "You are a naughty monkey.
  So I must put you
  in a cage."

He put Nicky in his cage
but Nicky did not like it.

One day Nicky got out of his cage.
He took Robert's cap
and he ran away with it.

Robert told Nicky
to put the cap down
but Nicky did not put it down.

He put it on his head
and he ran out on to the street.

Robert shouted:
  "Stop, you bad monkey."
But Nicky did not stop.

He ran and ran with Robert's cap
on his head.
Robert's daddy ran after Nicky
and stopped him.
Robert got his cap back.

Robert's daddy told Nicky
he was very bad.

27

Another day naughty Nicky got out
into the street and he saw a man
washing his car with a hose.

Nicky took the hose
and he put lots of water
on the man.

The man got very wet and
he did not like it.

The man took the hose
and he put lots of water on Nicky.
Nicky got very wet and
he did not like it.

The man took Nicky home and
he told Robert's uncle about him.

Robert's uncle said Nicky was
very bad.
He put him back in his cage.

Naughty Nicky got out
of his cage again
and he went up a tree.

Robert told Nicky to come down.
Robert's mummy came
and she told Nicky to come down.

Uncle Dick came and he said:
  "Where is Nicky?
  He is not in his cage."
Robert said:
  "He is up in the tree."

Then Uncle Dick said:
  "Nicky, come down at once."
But Nicky did not come down.

So uncle Dick took a ladder
and he went up the tree
and got Nicky.

He told Nicky he was
a very bad monkey
and he took him back to the house.

31

One day
Robert's mummy came home
with potatoes in her basket.
She put the basket down
and Nicky ran away with it.

He ran down the street and
all the potatoes fell out.
Robert's mummy said:
    "Put the potatoes back at once."

Nicky did what he was told
and Robert's mummy said he was
a good monkey now.